PETER THE GREAT MUSEUM OF ANTHROPOLOGY AND ETHNOGRAPHY, LENINGRAD

PETER THE GREAT MUSEUM OF ANTHROPOLOGY AND ETHNOGRAPHY, LENINGRAD

AURORA ART PUBLISHERS · LENINGRAD

Introduction
by Rudolf Its

Translated from the Russian
by Laura Souders

Layout and design
by Anatoly Kashirskikh

Photography by Alexander Gronsky
and Nikolai Kutovoi

© Aurora Art Publishers, Leningrad, 1989
Printed and bound in the USSR

$$M \ \frac{4904000000\text{-}748}{023(01)\text{-}89} \ 92\text{-}88$$

ISBN 5-7300-0044-8

Peter the Great's famous *Kunstkammer* (Cabinet of Curios) is located on the Spit of Vasilyevsky Island in Leningrad, not far from the main block of the University. It is one of the city's first stone buildings. Construction of the building intended as a museum began in 1718 and lasted ten years. Architects Georg Mattarnovi, Gaetano Chiaveri and Mikhail Zemtsov carried out construction according to Peter the Great's plans. In 1718, the three-storied stone palace rose above the Neva. Its middle section measures six stories high and is crowned with an annular sphere. The centre of nascent Russian science had museum halls which were very spacious in size and provided with numerous windows and lighting facilities.

The ideas of converting Russia into a mighty and educated state started taking shape in the last quarter of the seventeenth century.

Peter I wanted to model the first scientific institution on the European cabinets of curios. For advice on Russia's enlightenment and creation of a similar cabinet, Peter turned to the great mathematician and philosopher, Gottfried Leibniz. In a detailed answer Leibniz wrote: "Foreign works to be acquired should include diverse books, instruments, curiosities and rarities. All that may be circulated, that may be used for study. This calls for the creation of libraries, book shops, cabinets of curios and of natural and man-made objects as well as botanical and zoological gardens... Such a cabinet should contain all significant things and rarities created by nature and man. Particularly needed are stones, metals, minerals, wild plants and their artificial copies, animals, both stuffed and preserved in spirit, skeletons, pictures and reproductions of all that is unobtainable in its original form. Man-made pieces should be in the form of drawings, scale-models and copies of all sorts of successful inventions, metallic instruments, telescopes, mirrors, glassware, clocks, pictures, statues and sculptures, various models and antiquities. In short, all that could enlighten and please the eye."

In his programme for this collection, Leibniz gave preference to objects of both natural and technical sciences. But the Cabinet of Curios was created in Russia, a multinational country where the dissemination of knowledge about the culture, life and art of different peoples was of great social importance. That is why Peter I, while profiting from Leibniz's advice, placed in his museum natural and man-made objects from different areas of knowledge, from different regions of Russia and neighbouring countries.

The first exhibitions were based on Peter's personal collections of the rare items and instruments acquired during his foreign travels, as well as objects bought in Western European antique shops at his request. While in Amsterdam in 1698, the tsar himself purchased from the Dutch anatomist, Rys, a unique collection containing nearly 1,000 anatomical preparations, for the large sum of 30,000 guldens. In 1714, Peter I had his complete personal collections brought from Moscow to St. Petersburg. Artifacts of European and Asian origin, minerals, zoological and anatomical preparations were placed in a separate hall of the capital's Summer Palace, called The Cabinet of Curios, which was opened to visitors. Consequently, the year 1714 is considered the founding date of the first Russian museum, the precursor to practically all principal museums and institutions, including the Library of the Academy of Sciences.

The collections soon outgrew the premises of the Summer Palace and were transferred in 1719 to the two-storied mansion of boyar Kikin, who had fallen into disgrace. Meanwhile, on Vasilyevsky Island, construction had already begun for a special museum building.

Peter had intended the Spit of Vasilyevsky Island to be the centre of the new capital, but this idea was not fated to be realized. However, the location of the Kunstkammer on this site led, in time, to the formation of a major scientific and academic centre in St. Petersburg and the whole country.

The year 1724 marked the founding of the St. Petersburg Academy of Sciences. It incorporated the Kunstkammer that became the Academy's first and only scientific institution. Four years later, the collections which had grown enormously through personal donations from dignitaries and scholars, were transferred to a new building. In the 1730s, the ethnographical collection particularly increased as a result of acquisitions from the Second Kamchatka expedition.

The first Russian museum was still very young, when in the winter of 1739—40, Biron, the favourite of the cruel and quarrelsome Empress Anna Ioannovna, thought of organizing an "amusement wedding" between the court jester, Prince Mikhail Golitsyn, and his female counterpart, Avdotya Buzheninova, with a "procession of Russian peoples". An ice palace was built on the Neva, while the Kunstkammer was to distribute the priceless costumes of different Russian peoples for the courtiers' masquerade. This caused the museum huge losses. Shortly thereafter, in 1747, a great fire destroyed many collections and the upper tower, which was restored only two hundred years later. Until 1948, this unique architectural structure stood incomplete.

Having survived the "amusement wedding", the great fire and lengthy repairs after the fire, the museum was once again able to serve science. Its collections now embraced such branches as physics, mineralogy, anatomy, ethnography, zoology and botany, mechanics and chemistry, astronomy and geology. The geniuses of Russian science and engineering, Mikhail Lomonosov, Georg Richman, Andrei Nartov, Leonard Eyler and others, worked in this building during the eighteenth century. However, the head of the Academy's chancery and chief keeper of the Kunstkammer, Johann Taubert, was in no hurry to restore the expositions nor to sort out the stocks. In 1767, the great botanist, Samuel Gmelin, wrote to the President of the Academy: "I deeply regret that this Cabinet, which may signify more than all the treasures of the world, has now fallen into such a bad state, that it will hardly be possible to repair."

Gmelin's report produced an effect. On August 9th, 1767, posts were designated for museum curators. The four different departments were headed by eminent scientists of the time: Peter Pallas, Caspar Wolf, Samuel Gmelin and Ossip Petrov. With the exception of Petrov, who worked there only briefly, the remaining three became full members of the Academy and made a significant contribution to science. Thanks to them, the physico-topographical and ethnographical expeditions dispatched by the Academy from 1768 on, gathered material for the museum which succeeded in making up for the earlier losses.

In 1771, shortly after the appointment of the curators, the academician Semion Kotelnikov took the post of chief keeper of the Kunstkammer which he held for twenty-six years. The collection, which had grown considerably, was opened to the public. It's fame spread beyond Russia's borders and many considered it an honour to contribute to its further growth.

The museum's difficulties were aggravated by the death of Kotelnikov in 1797 and the departure of Ekaterina Dashkova, an outstanding figure of Russian culture, who retired from her post as President-Director of the Academy which she occupied from 1783 to 1796. The Kunstkammer was without a chief keeper for three years until the arrival of the academician Nikolai Ozeretskovsky. At one time Dashkova had given him a most flattering testimonial in supporting before the imperial court his expedition to the North of Russia. One of the remarkable events in the Kunstkammer's history is associated with Dashkova's name: the requisition of the costumes from the nobles which they had virtually appropriated since the "amusement wedding".

Assuming the directorship, Ozeretskovsky encountered a number of problems: funds and space lacked for housing the expanding collections, the former curator-academicians died and there was nobody to replace them; the University, established in conjunction with the Academy, virtually ceased to exist until its reopening in 1819.

In 1801, at the audience given by Alexander I on the occasion of his succession to the throne, the new keeper presented a report concerning the Kunstkammer's needs. The report remained unanswered for the ten years of his office. Nevertheless, Ozeretskovsky received constant support from various enlightened circles of Russian society and tried to do everything possible for the benefit of the Kunstkammer. At his request, the great seafarers, during their round-the-world voyages, kept a lookout for objects the museum needed, while diplomatic and trade missions sent gifts from other peoples and countries. Thanks to Ozeretskovsky, the Academy published a few of its works in Russian, including the Kunstkammer catalogue-guidebook by Ossip Beliaev which appeared in 1800.

Managing the Kunstkammer as a single scientific institution became difficult. The natural process of differentiation between the sciences necessitated the creation of separate Cabinets, independent of the museum. Thus in 1804, Ozeretskovsky organized the Mineralogical Cabinet and transferred its direction to the brilliant mineralogist, academician Vassily Severgin. On November 11th, 1818, the academician Christian Vren was appointed to head the Oriental Cabinet, a collection of eastern coins, manuscripts and books, which became known as the Asiatic Museum. In 1824, rich collections and books on botany formed the Botanical Department, which was headed by the academician Carl Trinius. The Egyptian Cabinet, or Egyptian Museum, was established on November 10th, 1825, where unique exhibits from Egypt, including mummies, were displayed. It was headed by the academician Feodor Graefe. Nikolai Ozeretskovsky died in 1827 and fate honoured him as the Kunstkammer's chief keeper.

In 1830, the Academy turned to the tsar with a request concerning the allocation of additional funds and space for the new institutions that had emerged within the museum. Nicholas I, however, decided to decrease staff and cancel the appointment of academicians as curators of departments. The tsar granted such meagre sums of money for the museum's maintenance, that the pride of Russian science was reduced to a warehouse of odd items, inaccessible for viewing and study. The Academy did not submit to such a decision and to make it known in higher circles of Russia, the administration distributed fifty copies of a petition to the tsar concerning the Kunstkammer's reorganization, hiring of new staff and allocation of funds. Correspondence and negotiations with the government lasted two years, arousing increasing public concern. Only five years later did the academicians' efforts yield concrete results. The year 1836 marked the official division of the Kunstkammer into seven museums: Mineralogical, Botanical, Zoological, Zootomical, Asiatic, Numismatic, Egyptian and Ethnographical. The Peter I Memorial Cabinet was formed separately. The museums' staff was to consist of both scientific and technical research workers. In 1837, after moving into two buildings neighbouring the Kunstkammer, the seven new museums opened their doors to the public.

The Mineralogical Museum became the foundation of the present-day Academy of Sciences Museum of the same name in Moscow. The Academy of Sciences Botanical Institute now incorporates the Botanical Museum. The Academy of Sciences Zoological Institute originated from the Zoological-Zootomical Museum. After transferring various objects from the Asiatic Museum to the Ethnographical, the remaining manuscripts and books served as the basis of what was to become the Academy of Sciences Institute of Oriental Studies. The Numismatic and Egyptian Museums were added to the Hermitage along with the Cabinet of Peter I (today's Gallery of Peter I). The Ethnographical Museum was the precursor to the Academy of Sciences Peter the Great Museum of Anthropology and Ethnography, as well as the Nikolai Miklukho-Maklay Institute of Ethnography. The year 1714 is generally considered the founding date of all the above-mentioned institutions.

Since the Museum of Anthropology and Ethnography moved to the Kunstkammer building, it has been often referred to as the Kunstkammer, but its own history began after the inauguration in 1837. The well-known linguist and ethnographer, Andrei Sjögren, was named the museum's first director in 1844. During his years in office, Sjögren encountered numerous problems. The ethnographical collections were transferred from the Kunstkammer to other Academy buildings located nearby on Customs Lane and Stock Exchange Passageway. However, space lacked for accommodating the several thousand exhibition pieces. It was, moreover, necessary to find the means to develop the growing centre of Russian ethnographical science.

In 1842, the Anatomical Cabinet was transformed by its head, academician Carl Baer, into the Museum of Somatic Anthropology and Pre-historical Archeology. Thus, within the Academy of Sciences there emerged yet another institution engaged in the study of Man, the stages of his development and early livelihood. The Department of Somatic Anthropology included a most valuable collection of archeological finds: implements; elegant antique sculptures of artistic workmanship made of gold, silver, stone and bronze; amulets and ornaments. The Department of Pre-historical Archeology had a direct link with the Ethnographical Museum, a link between the cultures of ancient and modern peoples.

The idea of uniting the two museums arose when the academician Anton Schiffner became director of the Ethnographical Museum. In 1860, Baer and Schiffner took active measures to create a single academic centre, a museum encompassing three fields of science: ethnography, anthropology and archeology. The Academy's needs, however, did not draw due attention and projects took a very long time to realize. The two museums were combined only in 1878, and at the proposal of the academician Leopold Schrenk — the eminent ethnographer-explorer of the peoples of the Amur and Far Eastern regions — this new institution was named the 'Museum of Anthropology and Ethnography Predominately of the Peoples of Russia'. The name was not entirely accurate, as the original ethnographical collections of Peter I included objects of daily life and culture not only from Russia, but from foreign countries as well. By the 1880s, the latter constituted a significant part of the museum's holdings. This is not surprising, as the eighteenth century is renowned for the Academy's expeditions throughout Russia, while the nineteenth century is noted for world voyages and expeditions to Russian America (Alaska), Oceania, Africa and South America.

Ten years thereafter, the Kunstkammer was finally given a first floor annex located on Customs Lane, as its ground floor had become overcrowded both for the employees and the collections. For years, exhibits remained packed and stored in cases, among which were priceless and unique objects from every continent. Thanks to the efforts of curator Fiodor Russov, a small section containing the rarest pieces was opened for public viewing in 1891.

In 1893, the famous orientalist Vassily Radlov was appointed director of the museum. In St. Petersburg by this time, the ethnographical department was already working under the auspices of the Russian Geographical Society. Ethnography also was part of the scientific disciplines studied at the universities of Moscow, St. Petersburg, Kazan and Tomsk. In Moscow, the Ethnographical Museum was operating, which had been founded by Dashkova. It contained, primarily, collections of Russian-made objects. In other words, the Museum of Anthropology and Ethnography was not the country's only centre for ethnographic studies, though it played a leading role in this field as an academic institution.

Radlov received a very valuable legacy but the possibilities of using it for science and education were meagre. The museum lacked personnel, a budget for financing expeditions and necessary exhibition space. Yet Radlov accomplished a great deal during his twenty-five years in office, constantly deriving support from progressive circles in Russia. Assessing his work, the prominent figure of Russian and, subsequently, Soviet ethnography, Lev Sternberg thus wrote in 1912: "In the past seventeen years, the Museum has quadrupled its exhibition space, expanded its collections by nearly twenty times and set out on the long road as a scientific institute of ethnography. In December 1902, in connection with St. Petersburg's Bicentennial the Museum received its present-day name as the 'Peter the Great Museum of Anthropology and Ethnography'. This name, which does not include Schrenk's words 'predominately of the peoples of Russia', reflects the character of the Museum's current activity. This is the museum of general ethnography, embracing the cultures of all mankind..."

In 1914, Radlov obtained the permission that the Academy of Sciences Library be gradually transferred from the Kunstkammer building and that the building itself be given to the museum. The museum made its final move there within the first five years after the October Revolution of 1917. Funds were also allocated for adding a second floor to the Kunstkammer's annex.

After the establishment of Soviet power, the museum's research fellows joined in active work for the cultural revival of outlying districts of former tsarist Russia. They travelled to distant regions, where they opened schools, helped to create written language and contributed in many ways to the development of national literatures. Numerous expeditions were organized and scientific works published. Up to the beginning of the Great Patriotic War (1941—1945), an average of forty thousand people visited the museum annually, which broke all records of attendance registered prior to the 1917 October Revolution. In 1933, the Academy of Sciences Institute of Anthropology and Ethnography was founded on the museum's basis. Shortly after, the word 'anthropology' was dropped from its name. But research in this field continued at the Institute of Ethnography which, since 1947, bears the name of the great Russian scientist and humanitarian, Miklukho-Maklay, in memory of his great services to ethnography.

The Moscow branch of the Academy of Sciences Institute of Ethnography was founded in 1943. Today, it is the leading institute both in number of research workers and in the problems they solve. Leningrad has basically maintained a historically established priority in the study of the Siberian, Oriental and Caucasian problems of ethnography. Contributing to this is one obvious advantage: the wealth of the museum's collections which represent a very significant scientific base.

The war brought difficult trials for the Kunstkammer staff. During the siege of Leningrad, having dispersed the most important collections throughout various sections of the city, the museum and the institute continued to carry out scientific research amidst the bombing and shelling. Despite cold and starvation, the staff guarded, while actually living in the depositories, the exhibitions entrusted to them. Very valuable collections were saved, costing the lives of thirty-three persons who perished during the blockade.

One thousand peoples are represented in the Museum of Anthropology and Ethnography by objects of material and spiritual culture, cult relics and articles of skilled craftsmen. The ethnographical collections, compiled during the last three centuries, preserve, as it were, the memory of its founders, the thoughts and hopes of people from different parts of the planet. In addition to the ethnographical collections, which today include more than 300,000 objects, the museum contains 500,000 archeological and 180,000 anthropological items.

The ethnographical collection traces its origin from 1716 when Peter I, while in Holland, purchased a large number of works from the chemist Albert Seba. The year before, he sent Lorenz Lang to Peking with the task of acquiring Chinese objects. Peter's work was continued by various people in Russia and abroad: scientists, travellers, dignitaries and commoners. Gifts were sent to the imperial family and to the Kunstkammer itself. After the Revolution, the inflow of gifts continued. The exchange of collections between the Museum of Anthropology and Ethnography and other museums in the world existed then as it still does today.

We will consider only the most important, most noteworthy entries. The eighteenth century occupies a special place in the history of the museum stocks' formation when Academy expeditions systematically and purposefully gathered material. The first real ethnographical collection was that of Daniel Messerschmidt, brought from Siberia and obtained by the Kunstkammer in 1727. Following that was a considerable number of objects donated by the participants of the Second Kamchatka Expedition (1733—43): Gerhard Miller, Johann Fischer, Johann Gmelin, Stepan Krasheninnikov and Georg Steller. It was namely these displays that suffered the heaviest damage in the great fire of 1747. Mikhail Lomonosov wrote in his memoirs that "the Siberian junk and clothing either burned in the fire or was damaged when thrown out of the blazing building onto the snow". Attempts to compensate for the losses were made in a short space of time. In 1753, the expedition of the Academy's physician, Franz Elachich, was dispatched to Peking with the task of collecting in China, as well as in Siberia, objects to replace those lost. By way of illustration, Elachich was given a detailed description of the one hundred and eighty Chinese objects with indications as to their material, appearance and size. Although Elachich was unable to purchase everything anew, he brought from China two hundred and seventy-three pieces. The Second Academy Expedition to Siberia (1768—74), which included Peter Pallas,

Samuel Gmelin and Ivan Georghi, was given an assignment similar to Elachich's.

In 1780, the Kunstkammer received James Cook's collection from Oceania, which substantially enriched the holdings of the respective section. In the late eighteenth and early nineteenth centuries, the American section took shape through round-the-world expeditions, acquisitions made by the Russian-American Company and through the transfer, in 1794, of Catherine II's personal Asian-American collection which she had received from the naval expedition led by Joseph Billings and Gabriel Sarychev. It was the beginning of a tradition following which all Russian seafarers considered a debt of honour to contribute gifts or to fulfil the museum's requests to gather exhibits.

In 1803, Ivan Kruzenstern and Yuri Lisiansky set out on the ships *Nadezhda* and *Neva* for a round-the-world voyage with instructions to supply the Kunstkammer with clothes and objects from the daily life of different European, Asian and American peoples: for the first time, they brought back wooden Aleutian hats, wooden combat helmets of the Tlingits and samples of Eskimo clothing. A catalogue was compiled based on this collection. From Vassily Golovnin's 1817—19 voyage on the sloop *Kamchatka*, the museum received a generous gift of objects illustrating the cultural and daily life of both the North and South American Indians. In 1819, Faddei Bellingshausen's and Mikhail Lazarev's famous Antarctic expedition departed from native shores. In 1828, the Kunstkammer received splendid exhibits from the far-away islands of the Pacific and Indian Oceans, as well as Australia. In 1826—29, the museum was presented with objects of Oceanic and American origin from the expeditions of Feodor Lithke on the sloop *Seniavin*. In 1833, the Kunstkammer obtained from the imperial chancery a unique collection which had been brought back from China by Mikhail Ladyzhensky, the colonel of the General Staff. He worked in Peking in 1830—31 at the diplomatic and ecclesiastical legations and collected over one thousand exhibits including clothes, items of worship and daily life, fabrics and objects of applied art. Thanks to Ladyzhensky, the Kunstkammer is the only museum in the world possessing the complete full-dress costume of a Chinese general, Prince of the Blood, who wore it once during the reign of the emperor, when the latter attended the great parade of guards.

In 1836, during the redistribution of collections between the museums, it became evident that a large part of the entries, although abundant, were disorderly and incomplete, particularly in the ethnographical, zoological and botanical collections from America. The Californian and North-Western Indians were poorly represented. In these conditions the Kunstkammer had to dispatch its own expedition to America. The academician Theodor Brandt, who was, in actual fact, director of the Museums of Zoology and Ethnography in 1839, and the academician Egor Schrader, curator of the Ethnography Museum, actively supported the idea. An approval was obtained from the Russian-American Company in July 1839 to help finance the expedition. Now it was necessary to find the person who would take on the task.

It was Ilya Voznesensky, a commoner by birth, an orphan who from five years of age was educated at the Kunstkammer. He learned to make zoological preparations and herbariae. During ten years spent in Russian America, Voznesensky collected and obtained six thousand items for the Zoological Museum, more than seven thousand for the Botanical Museum, almost one thousand for the Mineralogical, and more than one thousand for the Ethnographical. All collections were magnificently prepared, conserved and packed. One person accomplished a feat, having done in one time what would have normally taken several expeditions to do. In 1851, the Academy wrote to the tsar: "Voznesensky carried out the arduous assignment of the last expedition with complete success and self-devotion. The scientific results of this remarkable expedition, through its wealth, variety and importance, have surpassed all the Academy's expectations..." Then followed the request to appreciate Voznesensky's work, but as he was of the common people, "no education gave one the right to occupy class appointments". Nearly all his life Voznesensky was a pensioner of the Academy, deprived of the right to an official salary which he received only in his last years. In the history of the Kunstkammer and its museums, Voznesensky's work exceeds even the contributions of such world-renown scientists as Pallas, Krasheninnikov, Miklukho-Maklay and Kozlov.

In the mid-nineteenth century, on the Academy's assignment, academicians were in the field gathering collections: Leopold Schrenk on the Amur, professor Mathias Kastren in Western Siberia and Grigory Langsdorf in South America. The work of two prominent scientist-travellers and ethnographers, Vassily Junker and Nikolai Miklukho-Maklay, deserve particular mention. During the years 1875—78 and 1879—86, Junker worked in the inner regions of Africa, collecting objects of African material culture which today compose the main body of exhibits from this continent. Miklukho-Maklay voyaged to the Pacific Islands and lived for some time in New Guinea and Australia. In 1886, he donated to the museum a vast collection representing the Papuans and other peoples, in particular, the Rapanuans — who were the inhabitants of Easter Island — and the aborigines of Australia. Junker's collection numbered almost two thousand items and Miklukho-Maklay's, nearly one thousand.

While in 1890 the museum possessed 23,829 ethnographical items, in 1914 it already totalled 130,700. This considerable expansion was made possible thanks to the systematic gathering of collections representing the peoples of Russia, Asia (outside Russia), Africa and America, as well as through purchases from Russian and foreign collectors. In the early twentieth century, the museum received very important materials from Vassily Alexeyev, Alexei Ivanov and Peter Kozlov on China, Albert Frich on South America, Victor Anuchin on Western Siberia, Georgi and Liudmila Mervartov on India, etc.

After the 1917 October Revolution, many personal collections entered the museum together with collections assembled by the USSR Museum Reserve. Exchanges began with foreign museums. Although curtailed for a time, the exchanges were resumed in the 1950s and are still going on with museums in a number of countries, in particular Japan. In 1963 the Soviet diplomat Pavel Komin donated a collection illustrating the Papuan culture from West Irian.

During the Soviet period, the Kunstkammer's ethnographical collections have more than doubled, and today they rank first in the world (especially the collections representing non-European peoples).

Every museum section boasts a number of unique works which are the pride of Russian and Soviet ethnography. For example, in the Australia and Oceania section, apart from the beautifully carved wooden figurines of ancestors and sets of various objects of the Papuans brought back by Miklukho-Maklay, there are fine, elegant capes and cloaks made by the Hawaiians from the feathers of the birds Oo and Ii. There are also various items that belonged to the "Napoleon" of the Pacific, as was called Kameamea I, the founder and first king of the Hawaiian state (he presented them to James Cook). The American section contains Tlingit and Aleutian helmets, worked with great artistic mastery, from the Voznesensky collection. The African section displays the bronzes of Benin, the capital of the

Edo state which was burned by English colonists in 1897. Metal weapons and ivories of the inhabitants of tropical and southern Africa can also be seen. The Asian section (works of Asian origin outside the Soviet Union) possesses the largest and most refined collection of objects of applied and decorative arts. On display here are miniature Japanese netsuke, small Indian and Chinese sculptures of stone, bronze, wood and ivory, Chinese folk prints, Vietnamese embroidery, theatrical masks and figurines from Japanese and Indonesian puppet theatres, porcelain and ceramics from China, Japan and Korea. Found here are a unique portico from the palace in Nasik (India) and models of Hindu temples made from Sholo wood.

The peoples of the USSR, especially of Siberia and the North, are represented by traditional embroidery and patterned weaving, jewellery, embossed work, bone and wood carvings.

Before the Great Patriotic War of 1941—45, the annual attendance of the museum did not exceed 50,000. Today, from 300,000 to 500,000 Leningraders and tourists pass through its halls every year.

This art book includes the most important items from the artistic and scientific point of view. The layout corresponds to the museum's departments. It should be noted that the Kunstkammer building and its interiors reproduced in the book, belong to priceless monuments of architecture.

→
Detail of the original ceiling moulding in the ground floor interior.

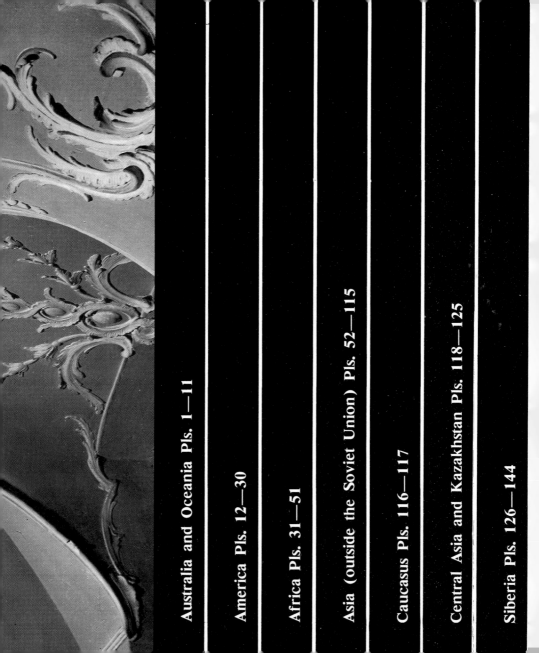

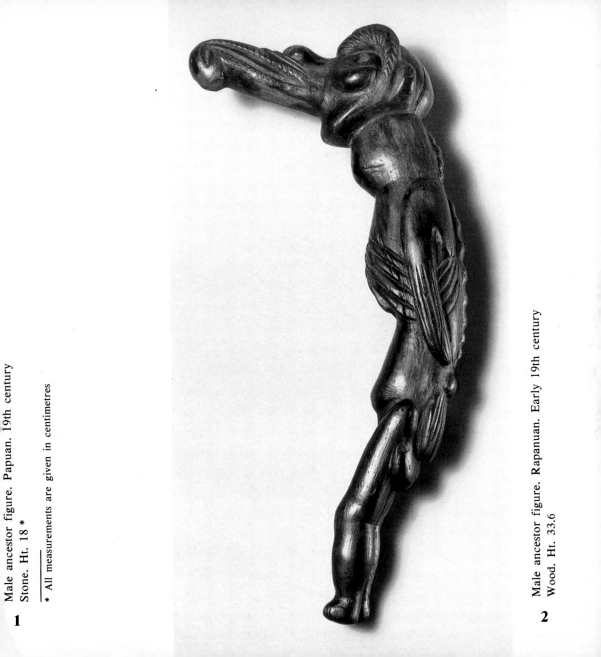

Male ancestor figure. Papuan. 19th century
Stone. Ht. 18 *

* All measurements are given in centimetres

Male ancestor figure. Rapanuan. Early 19th century
Wood. Ht. 33.6

1

2

3 Tablet with an inscription in Kokhau-rongo-rongo.
Rapanuan. Wood. 60×15

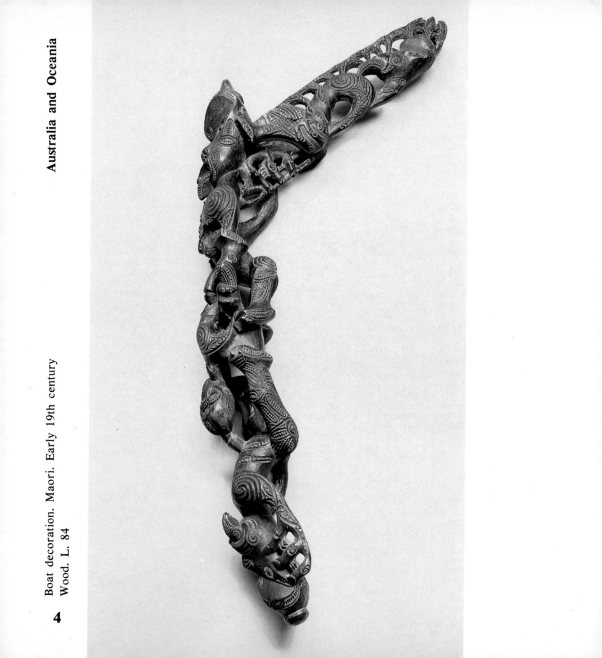

Boat decoration. Maori. Early 19th century
Wood. L. 84

4

Mask of a secret union's member. Melanesia. Early 20th century
Wood. 53×21 **5**

6 Bench/head-rest. Polynesia. 18th century
Wood. 52×17

Ceremonial axe. Polynesia. Late 19th century
Wood. 49 × 13 × 7

7

Boomerang. Australia. 19th century
Wood. 52 × 4.5

8

Helmet. Hawaii. 18th century
Oo and Ii birds' feathers. Ht. 30 **9**

10 Ceremonial paddle. Polynesia. Early 19th century
Wood. 128×48×30

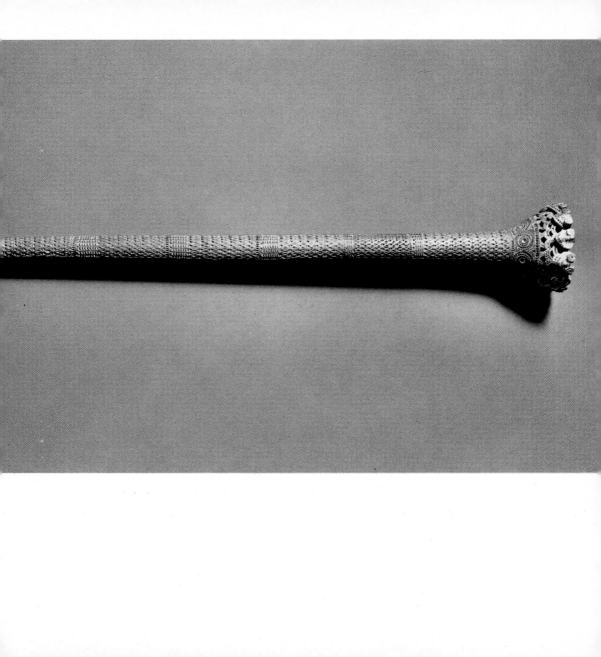

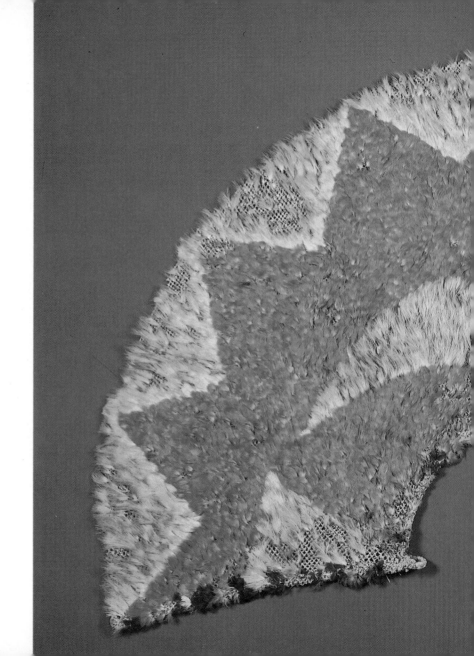

Cape. Hawaii. 18th century
Oo and Ii birds' feathers. 180×30

11

12 Vessel. Tlingit. Mid-19th century
Pine wood. Ht. 12

Dance headdress of a shaman. Tlingit. First half 19th century
Cedar wood. L. 50   **13**

Shaman rattle. Tlingit. Late 19th century
Cedar wood. 29×13×10.5

14

15 Helmet-mask. Tlingit. First half 19th century
Cedar wood. 35×30

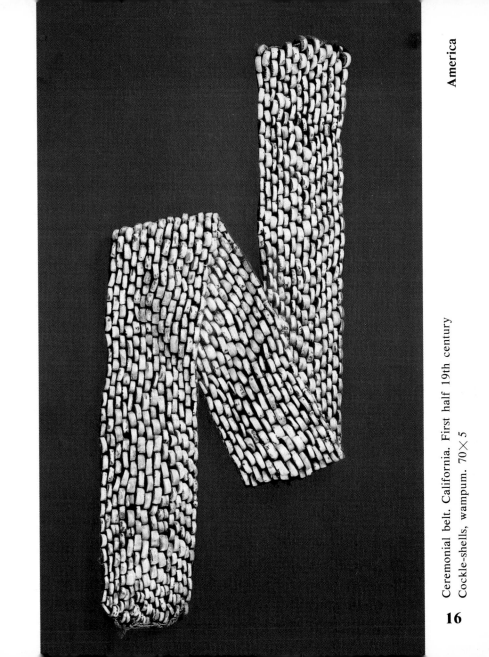

Ceremonial belt. California. First half 19th century
Cockle-shells, wampum. 70 × 5

Cloak. California. First half 19th century
Crow feathers. L. 140

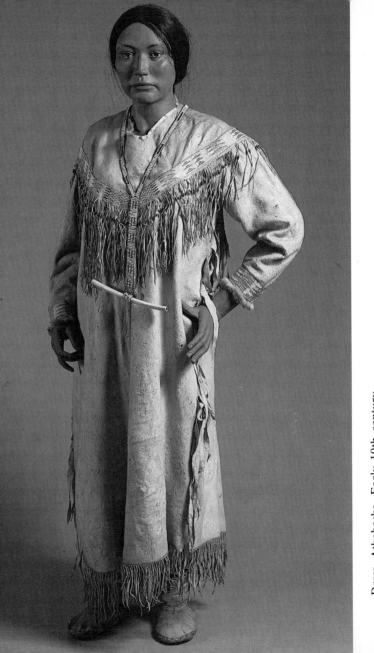

Dress. Athabaska. Early 19th century
Deerskin trimmed with porcupine quills. L. 150

18

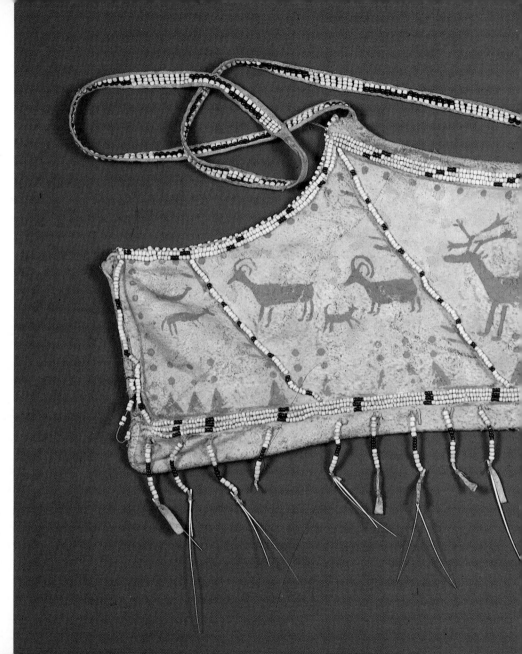

Quiver. Athabaska. Mid-19th century
Deerskin trimmed with beads. L. 77

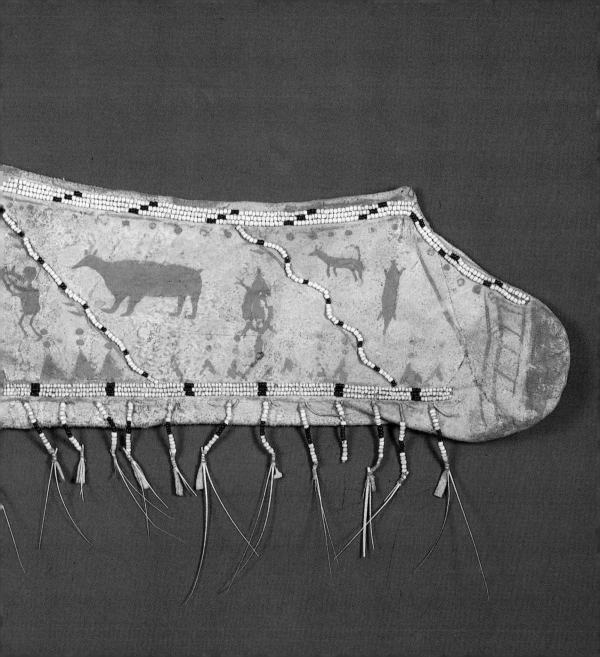

20 Winged object. Ancient inhabitants of the Bering Sea coast area; from Ekven burial ground (Chukot Peninsula). 1st century B. C. Walrus ivory. 21 × 5

Mask. Ancient inhabitants of the Bering Sea coast area;
from Ekven burial ground (Chukot Peninsula). 2nd—3rd centuries.
Wood. 23×18

21

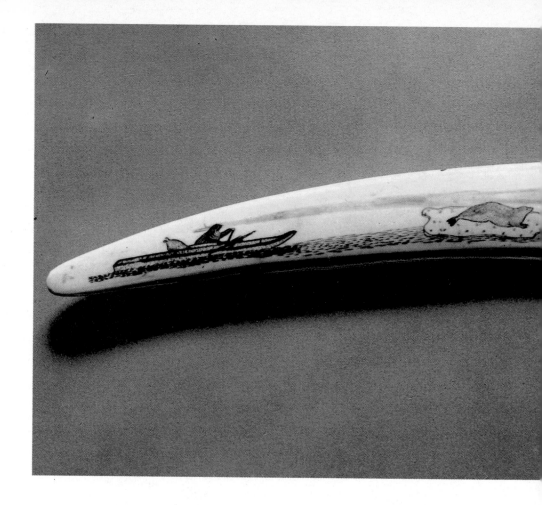

22 Engraving on walrus tusk. Eskimo. 20th century
L. 50

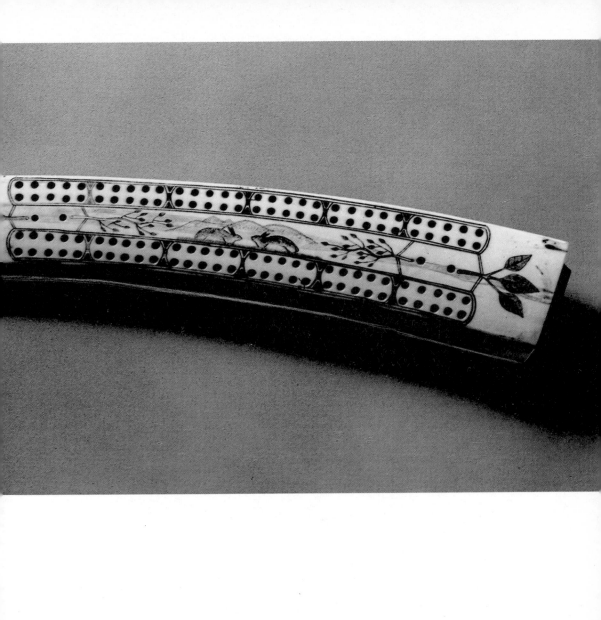

Figure of a woman. Eskimo. Early 19th century
Wood. Ht. 15

23

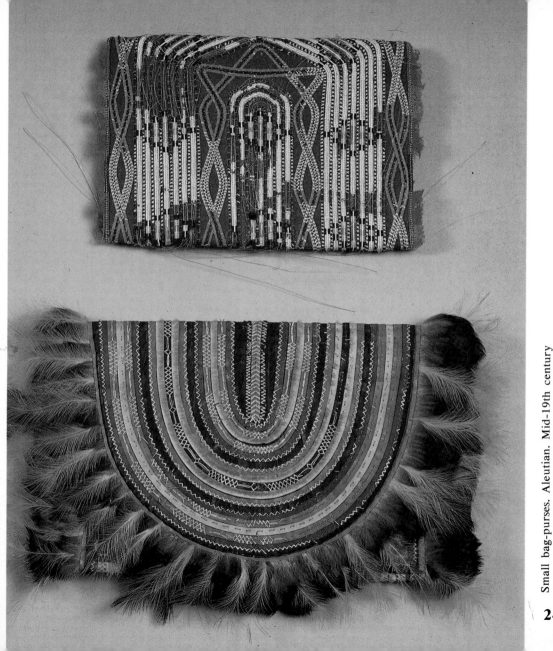

Small bag-purses. Aleutian. Mid-19th century
Leather, beach grass (Elumus mollis), feathers. 12×18 and 10×15

24

Funeral mask. Aleutian.
25 Mid-19th century
Wood. 28×26

Figure of a man. Aleutian.
19th century **26**
Mammoth bone trimmed with beads.
9×6

27 Hunting headdress. Aleutian. 19th century
Wood, ivory. 30×15

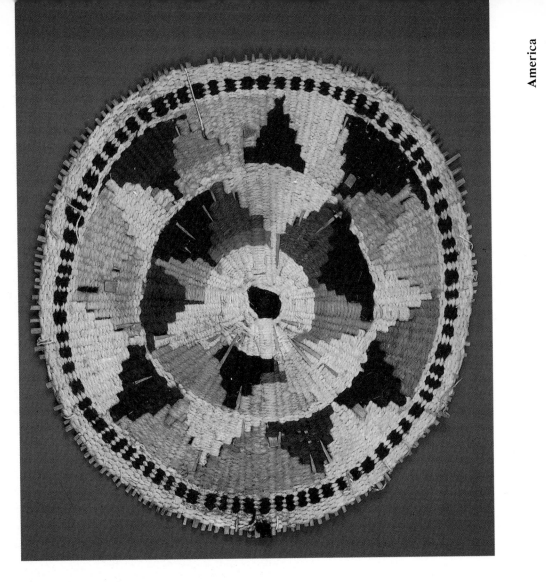

Ritual shield. Huichol Indians, Mexico. Late 19th century
Bamboo woven with coloured wool thread. Diameter 53

29 Appliqué decoration for shirt.
Cunha Indians, Panama.
20th century
Cotton. 51 × 37

America

30 Apron. Oyana, French Guyana. Early 20th century
Tapa bark, corals, tubular shaped bones. 116×58

Plaque with a relief figure of a courtier. Benin.
17th—18th centuries
Bronze. 43×18

31

Africa

Rooster. Benin. 17th—18th centuries
Bronze. Ht. 52

32

Head of a woman. Benin. 17th—18th centuries
Bronze. Ht. 47.5, base diameter 23.5

33

Figure of a man. Cameroun. 19th century
Bronze. Ht. 12

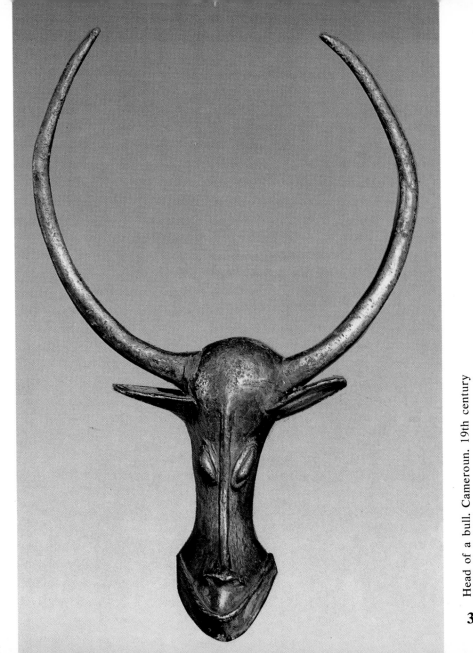

Head of a bull. Cameroun. 19th century
Bronze. Ht. 17

35

Pipe. Cameroun. 19th century
Bronze. L. 54

36

Paint container. Azande, Congo. 19th century
Wood. Ht. 50

37

Ritual figurines. Basongo. Congo. 19th century
Wood. Ht. 20.5 and 18

38

Ritual figurine. Mpongwe, Gabon. 19th century
Wood, cape made from vegetable fibre. Ht. 51

39

40 Basket. Ziba. 19th century
Bamboo. Ht. 16, diameter 28

Mask. Botswana. 19th century
Wood. Ht. 40 **41**

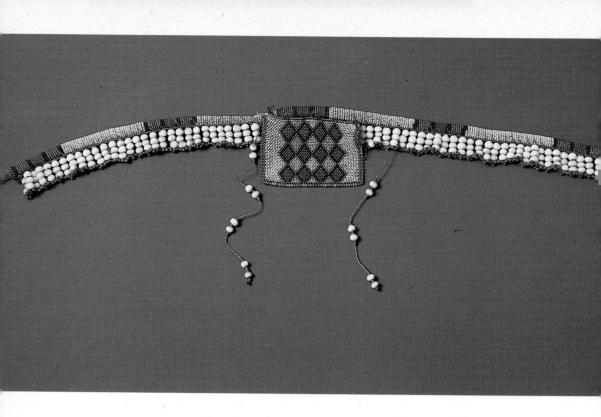

42 Apron-belt. Khosa. 19th century
Beadwork. 68×9

Africa

Combs, hairpins. Anyang, Mpongwe, Amhara. 19th century
Wood. 24, 15.5, 16, 37.5 and 15

43

44 Pipe bowl. Bali. 19th century
Painted clay. 13×12

Neck decoration. Zulu. 19th century
Beadwork. L. 62

45

Spoon. Congo. 19th century
Wood. L. 17

Ritual figurine. Bambara. 19th century
Wood. Ht. 56

48

Stool. Azande, Congo. 19th century
Wood. Ht. 17.5 **49**

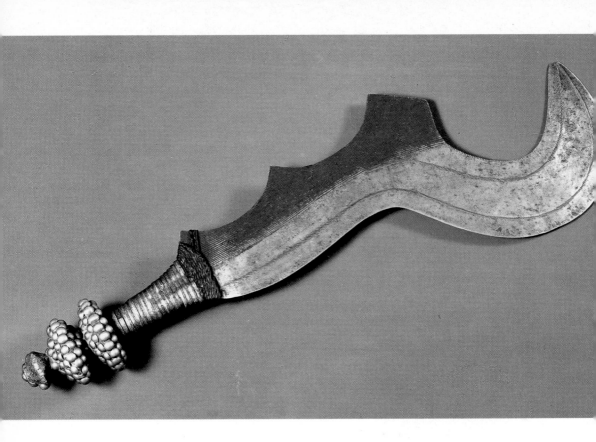

50 Ceremonial knife. Congo. 19th century
Iron, copper wire and inlays. L. 64

Headdress. Bamana. 19th century
Bambo (base), wood (animal carving), animal tails
(upper decoration). 70×20

51

Figure of a woman. Japan. 18th century
Porcelain. Ht. 44

Ikebana pot. Japan. 18th century
Porcelain. Ht. 5.2, diameter 20.3 **53**

54 Vases. Japan. 19th century
Faience. Ht. 12 (of each)

Bowl. Japan. 18th century
Porcelain. Ht. 4.1, diameter 14.9 **55**

56 Small plate. Japan. 18th century
Metal, lacquer, mother-of-pearl inlays. Diameter 24.5

Netsuke. Japan. 19th century
Ivory. Ht. 4.5

58 Sword. Japan. 19th century
Ivory. L. 37.8

59 Dish. Japan. 19th century
Wood, lacquer, ivory inlays. Diameter 36.5

Picnic set. Japan. 19th century
Lacquer, gold painting. 22.6×24×14.9 **60**

Mask for folk holidays (animal's muzzle). Japan.

61 19th — early 20th centuries

Wood, fell, horse-hair, oil paint. 31×39

Brush stand. Japan. 19th century
Ivory. 11.3×5.1

Model of a junk. China. 19th century
Bamboo. 20 × 40

Helmet. China. 19th century
Metal, silver trim. Ht. 35, diameter 27

64

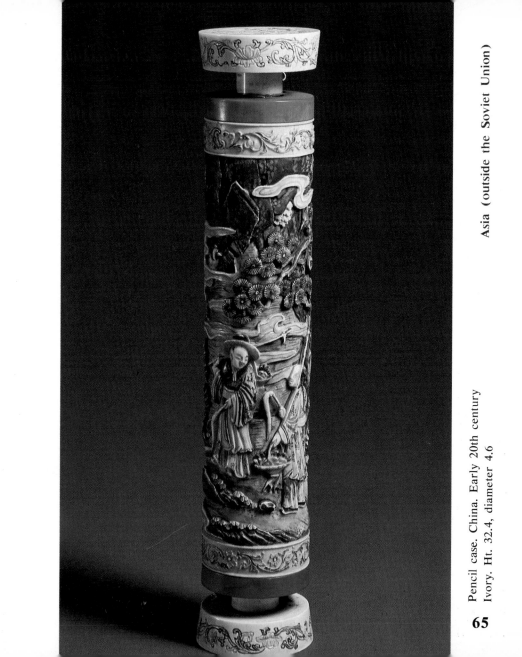

Pencil case. China. Early 20th century
Ivory. Ht. 32.4, diameter 4.6

Asia (outside the Soviet Union)

65

66 Goblet. China. Late 19th century
Bamboo. Ht. 15, diameter 12

Bowl. China. Early 17th century
Porcelain. Ht. 9.1, base diameter 8.7 **67**

Figurine of a monk. China. 19th century
Bronze. Ht. 17.8

Asia (outside the Soviet Union)

Peacock. China. Early 18th century
Copper, enamel. Ht. 28.6 **69**

Vase-candlesticks. China. 19th century
Porcelain. Ht. 24 (of each)

70

Vase. China. 15th century
Porcelain. Ht. 40.6

Vessel. China. 19th century
Bronze. Ht. 31

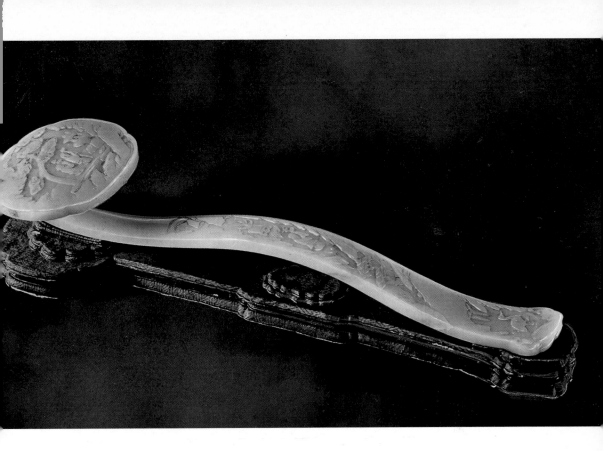

Staff for well-wishing ceremonies. China. 19th century
Nephrite. L. 72.2 **73**

74 Diadem. China. Early 19th century
Silver, kingfisher feathers. 11×6

Hairpin. China. Early 19th century
Silver, kingfisher feathers. 17×14

Asia (outside the Soviet Union)

Box. China. 19th century
Lacquer, mother-of-pearl inlays. 17.5 × 43.5 × 24.5

76

Lidded bowl. China. 19th century
Nephrite. Ht. 11.6, base diameter 8.4   77

Pagoda (model). China. Early 19th century
Ivory. Ht. 26.5, base width 8

78

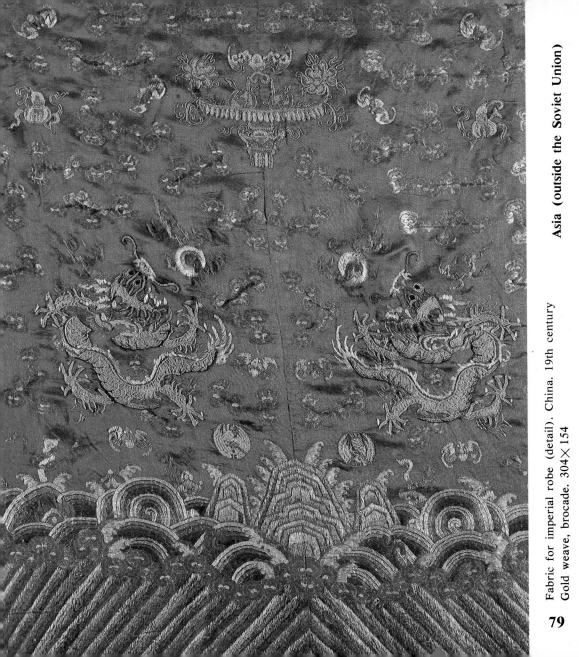

Fabric for imperial robe (detail). China. 19th century
Gold weave, brocade. 304×154

Asia (outside the Soviet Union)

80 Incense burner. China. Late 18th century
Bronze. L. 52.2

Figurine of a monk. China. 19th century
Porcelain. Ht. 22

Asia (outside the Soviet Union)

82 Mask for a Zam mystery. Mongolia. 19th century
Wood. 36.1×35

Buddha. Mongolia. 19th century
Bronze. Ht. 21.1 **83**

84 Bowl. Korea. 11th—12th centuries
Celadon. Ht. 11.2, base diameter 7.6

Vase. Korea. 14th—15th centuries
Crackle-faience. Ht. 37.2, base diameter 12.9

Asia (outside the Soviet Union)

86 Incense burner. Korea. 15th—16th centuries
Copper, silver. Ht. 17.1, diameter 21

Small chest. Korea. 19th century
Lacquer, mother-of-pearl inlays. 40.5×23.1×14   **87**

Screen. Korea. By Choun Song (1676—1759)
Silk. 84×304

Asia (outside the Soviet Union)

89 Teapot. India. 19th century
Copper. Ht. 23, base diameter 12

Helmet. India. 19th century
Copper. Diameter 63

91 Dish. India. 19th century
Steatite, semi-precious stones. Diameter 29.5

Shiva. India. Early 20th century
Sandalwood. Ht. 20

92

93 Bowl. Ceylon. Early 20th century
Coconut shell. Ht. 10.5, diameter 13

Portico. Nasik, Maharashtra, India. 17th century
Teak wood

Woman's bracelet. Ceylon. 20th century
Silver, ruby, leucosapphire. 6×3

Batik. Sunda, Indonesia. 19th century
Cotton decorated with batik. 105×250

Model of a boat. Bengal, India. Early 20th century
Ivory. 45×17.3

Puppet of the *wajang-golek* theatre. Java, Indonesia.
19th century
Wood, cloth. Ht. 62

98

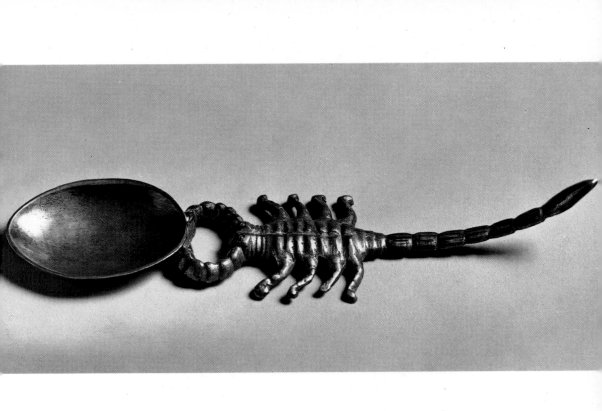

Spoon. Java, Indonesia. 20th century
Bronze. L. 15 **99**

Bell. Java, Indonesia. Early 14th century
Bronze. Ht. 17.5, diameter 11.5

Shiva. Java, Indonesia. 14th century
Stone. Ht. 68

101

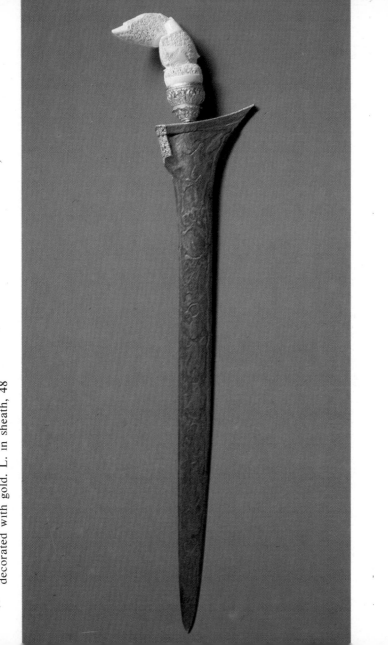

Kris, sheathed dagger. Sumatra, Indonesia. 19th century
Ivory (hilt), damascened steel (dagger), wooden sheath
decorated with gold. L. in sheath, 48

102

Woman's wedding knife. Dayaki. Late 19th century
Bronze. L. 26.5 **103**

Horn for holding poisonous drugs. Batak. Sumatra,
Indonesia. 19th century
Goat's horn decorated with silver, wooden cover. L. 25

104

Asia (outside the Soviet Union)

Pair of cult figures. Bali, Indonesia. Late 19th century
Wood. Ht. 52 and 47

105

Figurine of "Mother of Rice". Bali, Indonesia.
Early 20th century
Lontari palm leaves. Ht. 44

106

Idols. Nias, Sumatra, Indonesia. Early 20th century Asia (outside the Soviet Union)
Wood, cotton fabric. Ht. 23.5, 16 and 20

107

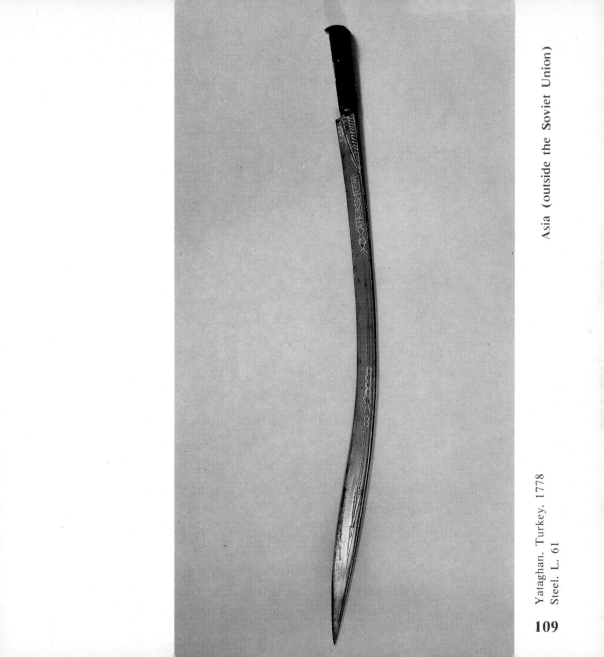

Asia (outside the Soviet Union)

Yataghan. Turkey. 1778
Steel. L. 61

109

Coffee set. Turkey. Early 20th century
110 Metal (coffeepot), porcelain and copper (cup with holder)
and copper (container for water). Ht. 11.5, 3.7, 3.3 and 10.4

Vessel. Persia. 19th century
Metal, glass, turquoise. Ht. 41

Asia (outside the Soviet Union)

111

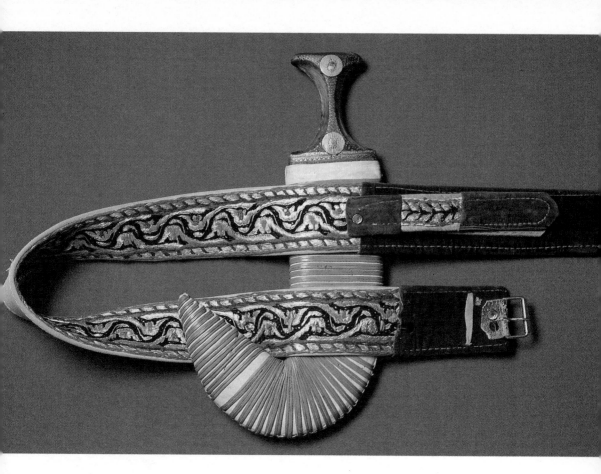

Kalamkar, wedding spread.
112 Persia. Early 20th century
Printed canvas. 305×160

Sheathed dagger and belt.
Arab. Yemen. 20th century
Steel (dagger), wood (hilt),
horn (sheath), leather and
cloth (belt). L. of dagger **113**
in sheath, 47.1. L. of belt, 108

Child's leg bracelets. Arab, Yemen.
114 20th century
Silver. Diameter 5.3

Screen for wedding (detail).
Halmahera, Indonesia.
19th century
Screw-pine leaves, mother-of-pearl. **115**
66×182

116 Oil lamp. Village of Kubachi, Daghestan. 19th century Bronze. 8×23

Men's Sunday shirt. Khevsur. 19th century Velvet, wool, gold needlework, **117** beads. 89×46

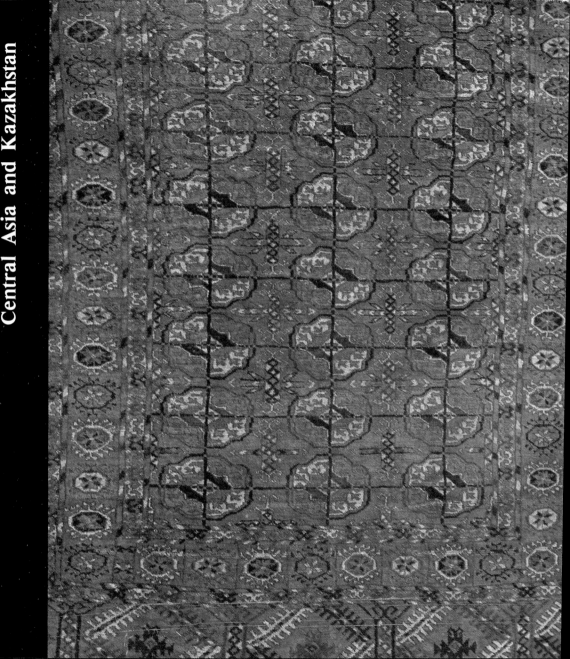

Central Asia and Kazakhstan

Rug (detail). Turkmen. 19th century
Wool

118

Saddle-girth (detail). Turkmen. Early 20th century
Wool. 12×105

119

120 *Kse*, men's belt. Kazakh. 19th century
Leather, metal, cornelian. 105×24

Saukele, wedding headdress. Kazakh. 19th century
Velvet, silk, metal, cornelian, coral. 160×25

Fabric samples (details). Uzbek. 19th century
Silk, velvet

Central Asia and Kazakhstan

Bedspread (detail). Uzbek. 19th century
Silk. 300×400

124 Saddle-cloth. Uzbek. 19th century
Velvet. 79 × 119

Small table. Uzbek. 19th century
Walnut, mother-of-pearl inlays. 71 × 40

125

126 Finial. Scythian, Tuva. 5th—4th centuries B. C.
Gold, turquoise, cornelian. Ht. 4

Walrus and seals. Chukchi. 19th century
Walrus ivory. 9×7; 10×5

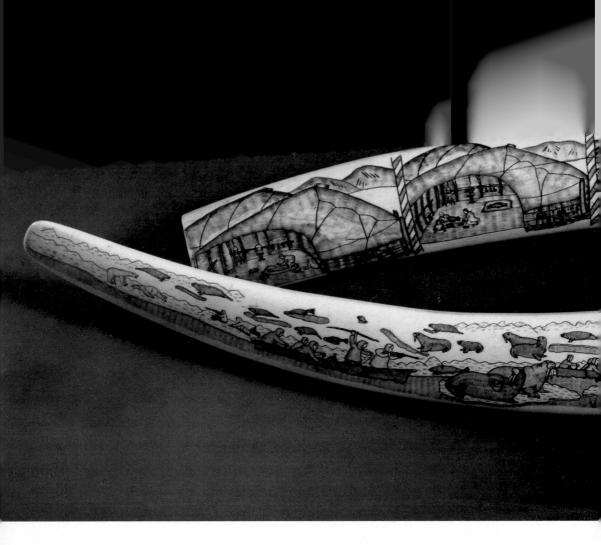

128 Engraving on walrus tusk. Chukchi. Early 20th century
L. 70

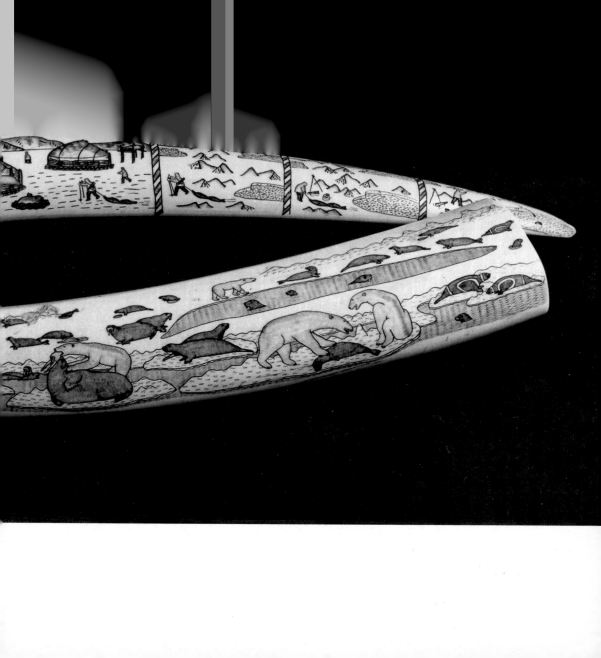

Yak, goat lying and black goat. By Oyoup and Khuna.

129 Tuvinian. 20th century

Agalmatolite. Ht. 10, 4.5 and 9

Carved walrus tusk. Eskimo. Early 20th century
L. 70 **130**

Sheath for woman's knife, child's shin-pad. Khanty.
131 19th and early 20th century
Birch bark, deerskin. 21×6 and 14×14.5

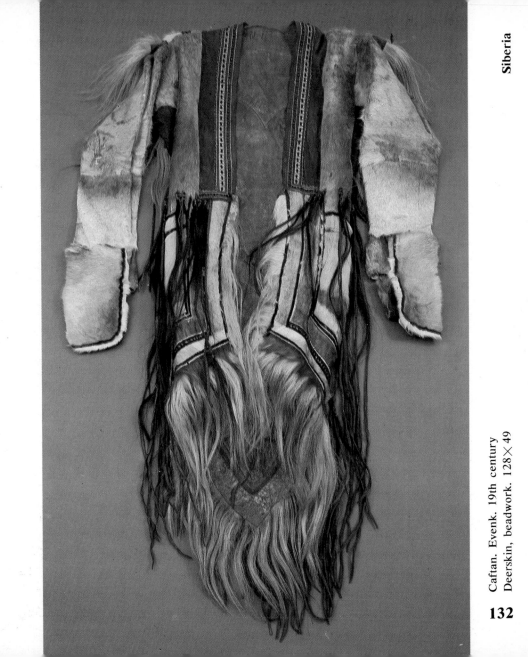

Caftan. Evenk. 19th century
Deerskin, beadwork. 128 × 49

Model of a Yakut farmstead. Yakut. 19th century
Bone. 93×59

133

Box. Neghidal. 19th century
Birch bark, stamped designs. Ht. 25, diameter 14.5

Saddle-cloth. Yakut. 19th century
Cloth, leather. 86×54 **135**

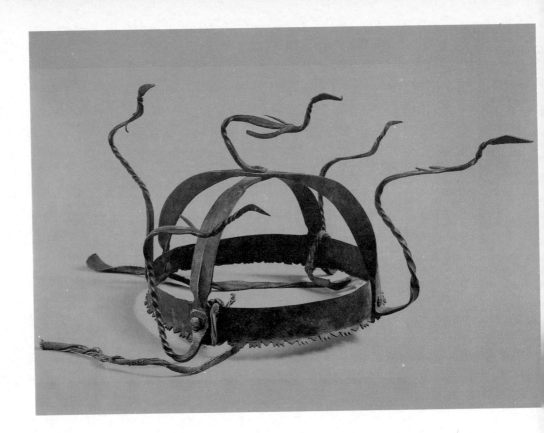

136 Shaman crown. Ket. Mid-19th century
Metal. Ht. 19, diameter 18

Parka. Nganasan. 19th century
Deerskin. 85×48 **137**

138 Ladle for the bear festival. Nivkhi. 19th century
Wood. 98×13

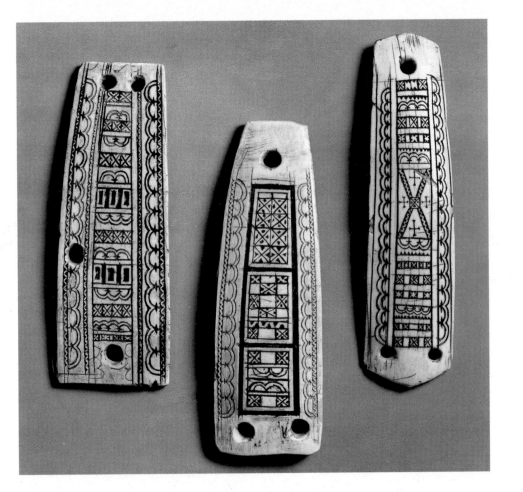

Siberia

Cheekpieces. Evenk. 19th century
Mammoth ivory. 17×6 and 18×5

139

Braidpieces. Khanty. 19th century
Beadwork. L. 28

140

Temple decorations. Buriat. 19th century
Silver, corals, malachite. 12.5 and 11.5 **141**

Mask. Buriat. 19th century
Copper. 30 × 25

142

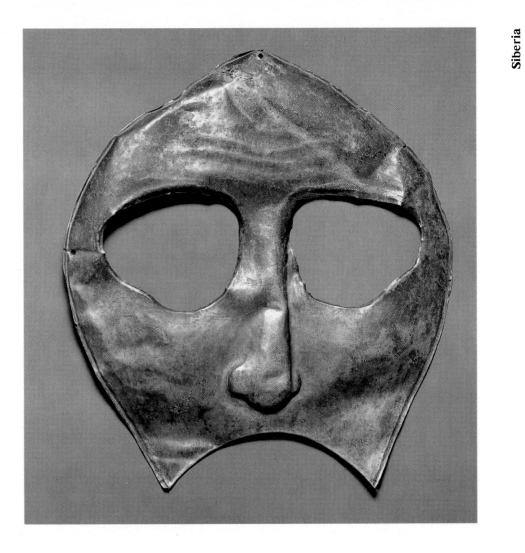

Siberia

Mask. Evenk. Early 19th century
Copper. 30×34 **143**

Sledge. Kamchadal.
18th century **144**
Wood, leather. 210×70

145 Bracelet. Bulgaria. Mid-19th century
Silver. Ht. 4, diameter 6

Comb. Bulgaria. 19th century
Silver. L. 14.5 **146**

Wine flask. Hungary. 19th century
Ceramic. 16×12

Gingerbread. Poland. 20th century
Dough. 17×9 **148**

149 Woman's waistbelt decoration. Mordvinian. 20th century
Cotton, metal, beads, cockle-shell. 63×46

Lace. Russia. 20th century
Cotton thread **150**

151 Ladle. Russia. 1758
Silver. 26×14×16

Bird. Russia. 19th century
Fir wood. 51×49 **152**

153 Small chest. Russia. 20th century
Birch wood, ivory. 12 × 22 × 14

154 Weathercock. Russia. 19th century
Metal, wood. 53×42

МУЗЕЙ АНТРОПОЛОГИИ И ЭТНОГРАФИИ ИМЕНИ ПЕТРА ВЕЛИКОГО

Альбом (на английском языке)

Издательство „Аврора". Ленинград. 1989

Изд. № 1459. (4-50)

ЛПО «Типография имени Ивана Федорова»

Printed and bound in the USSR